THE LITTLE HOUSE BOOKS

*T*he Little House books tell the story of Laura Ingalls, a little girl who lived during the time of the settling of the American frontier. The books describe how Laura and her family traveled by covered wagon from the Big Woods of Wisconsin across the western frontier, finally settling in the town of De Smet, South Dakota.

The Little House books are a wonderful adventure story. But they are even more exciting because they are based on author Laura Ingalls Wilder's own childhood. Laura and her Pa, her Ma, and her sisters Mary, Carrie, and Grace really did live in all the little houses described in her books. Laura wrote the Little House books when she was a grown woman, basing them on memories of her days as a young pioneer girl.

My Little House Diary is a place for you to record all of your secret hopes and dreams, and your private thoughts about your family and friends, your schooldays, and most of all, yourself.

January

The little log house was almost buried
in snow. Great drifts were banked against the
walls and windows, and in the morning
when Pa opened the door, there was a wall
of snow as high as Laura's head.

—LITTLE HOUSE IN THE BIG WOODS

February

The whole house smelled good, with the sweet and spicy smells from the kitchen, the smell of the hickory logs burning with clear, bright flames in the fireplace, and the smell of a clove-apple beside Grandma's mending basket on the table.

—LITTLE HOUSE IN THE BIG WOODS

March

They were happy as they drove through the

springtime woods. Carrie laughed and bounced, Ma was

smiling, and Pa whistled while he drove the horses.

The sun was bright and warm on the road. Sweet, cool

smells came out of the leafy woods.

—LITTLE HOUSE IN THE BIG WOODS

April

Birds sang in the leafing hazel bushes

along the crooked rail fence. The grass grew green

again and the woods were full of wild flowers.

Buttercups and violets, thimble flowers and tiny starry

grassflowers were everywhere.

—Little House in the Big Woods

May

In the mornings they ran through the dewy

chill grass that wet their feet and dabbled the hems of their

dresses. They liked to splash their bare feet through

the grass all strung with dewdrops. They liked to watch

the sun rise over the edge of the world.

—ON THE BANKS OF PLUM CREEK

June

They had playhouses under the two big oak trees

in front of the house. Mary's playhouse was under Mary's

tree, and Laura's playhouse was under Laura's tree.

The soft grass made a green carpet for them. The green

leaves were the roofs, and through them they

could see bits of the blue sky.

—Little House in the Big Woods

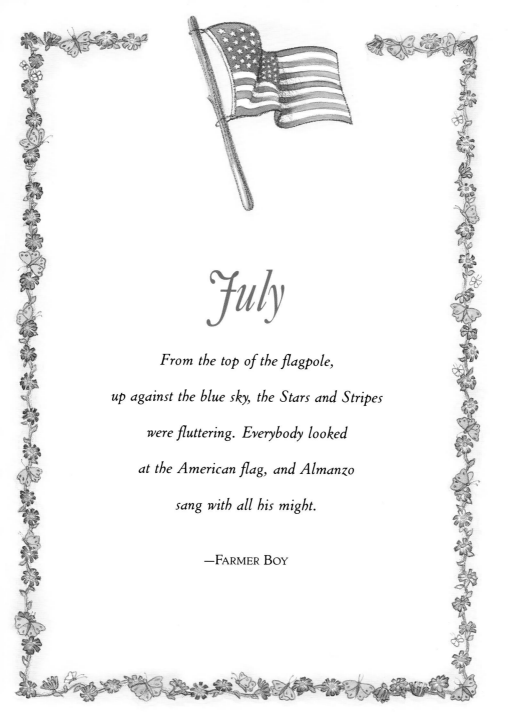

July

From the top of the flagpole,

up against the blue sky, the Stars and Stripes

were fluttering. Everybody looked

at the American flag, and Almanzo

sang with all his might.

—FARMER BOY

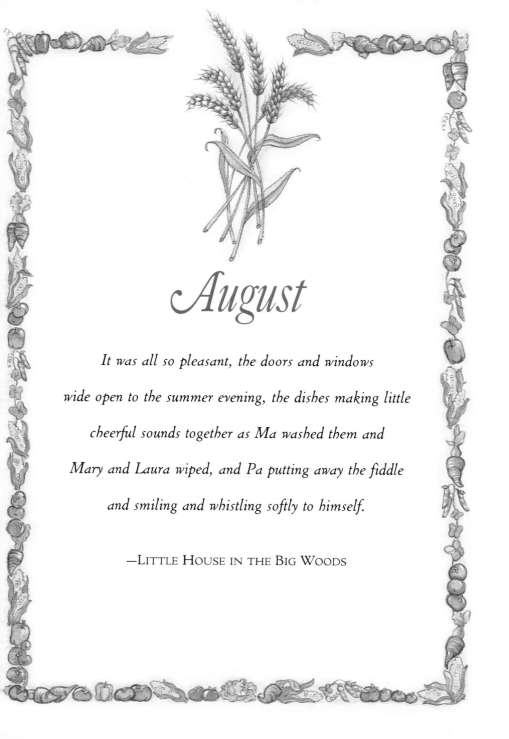

August

It was all so pleasant, the doors and windows
wide open to the summer evening, the dishes making little
cheerful sounds together as Ma washed them and
Mary and Laura wiped, and Pa putting away the fiddle
and smiling and whistling softly to himself.

—LITTLE HOUSE IN THE BIG WOODS

September

Outside, the night was large and full

of stars. Pa sat for a long time in the doorway

and played his fiddle and sang

to Ma and Mary and Laura in the house

and to the starry night outside.

—LITTLE HOUSE ON THE PRAIRIE

October

Acorns were falling from the oaks,
and Laura and Mary made little acorn cups and saucers
for the playhouses. Walnuts and hickory nuts were
dropping to the ground in the Big Woods, and squirrels
were scampering busily everywhere, gathering their winter's
store of nuts and hiding them away in hollow trees.

—LITTLE HOUSE IN THE BIG WOODS

November

Often the wind howled outside
with a cold and lonesome sound. But in the
attic Laura and Mary played house with
the squashes and the pumpkins, and
everything was snug and cosy.

—LITTLE HOUSE IN THE BIG WOODS

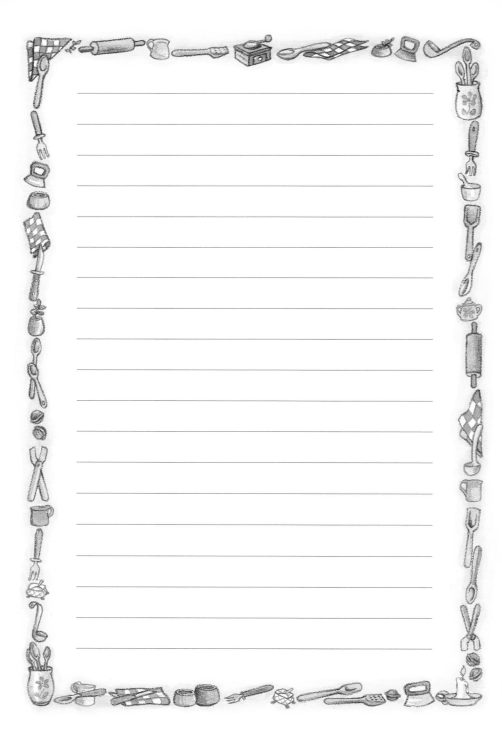

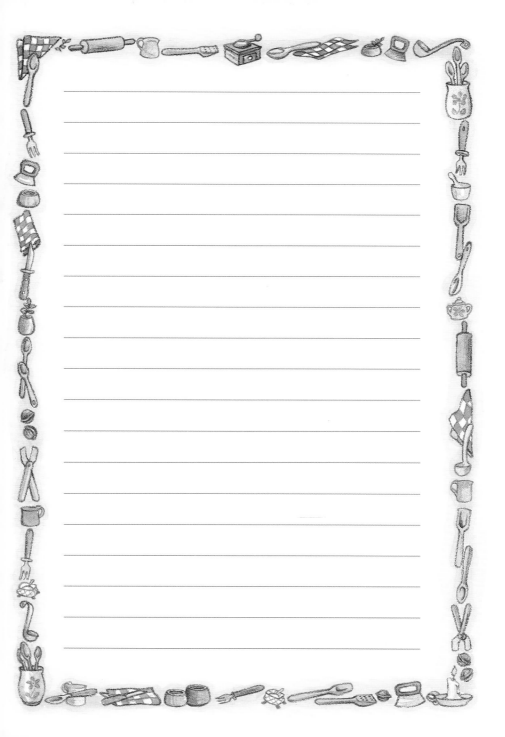

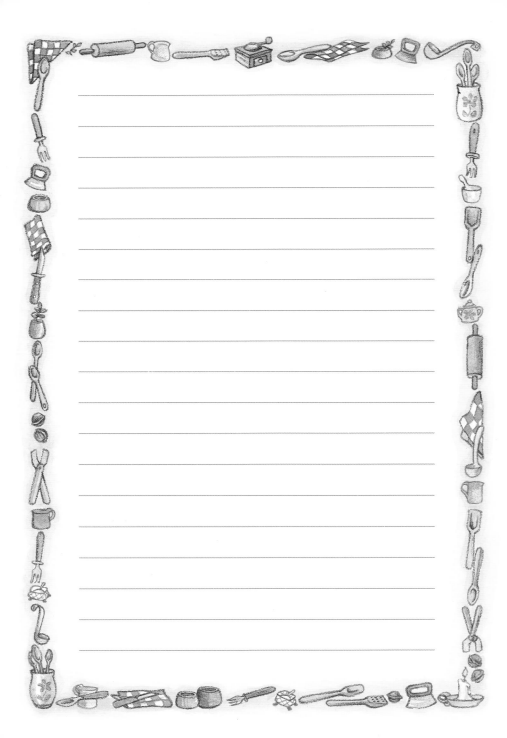

December

The kitchen was full of delicious smells.

Newly baked bread was cooling, frosted

cakes and cookies and mince pies and pumpkin

pies filled the pantry shelves, cranberries

bubbled on the stove.

—FARMER BOY